George Jacob Holyoake

The principles of secularism

George Jacob Holyoake

The principles of secularism

ISBN/EAN: 9783743317956

Manufactured in Europe, USA, Canada, Australia, Japa

Cover: Foto ©Lupo / pixelio.de

Manufactured and distributed by brebook publishing software
(www.brebook.com)

George Jacob Holyoake

The principles of secularism

THE

Principles of Secularism

𝕴llustrated.

BY GEORGE JACOB HOLYOAKE.

"Do the duty nearest hand,"—*Goethe.*

[THIRD EDITION, REVISED.]

LONDON:

BOOK STORE, 282, STRAND ;

AUSTIN & CO., 17, JOHNSON'S COURT, FLEET STREET.

1870

"If you think it right to differ from the times, and to make a stand for any valuable point of morals, do it, however rustic, however antiquated, however pedantic it may appear ; do it, not for insolence, but seriously—as a man who wore a soul of his own in his bosom, and did not wait till it was breathed into him by the breath of fashion."—THE REV. SIDNEY SMITH, Canon of St. Paul's.

CONTENTS.

INTRODUCTORY.

CHAPTER I.

N a passage of characteristic sagacity, Dr. J. H. Newman has depicted the partisan aimlessness more descriptive of the period when this little book first appeared, sixteen years ago, than it is now. But it will be long before its relevance and instruction have passed away. I therefore take the liberty of still quoting his words :—

"When persons for the first time look upon the world of politics or religion, all that they find there meets their mind's eye, as a landscape addresses itself for the first time to a person who has just gained his bodily sight. One thing is as far off as another ; there is no perspective. The connection of fact with fact, truth with truth, the bearing of fact upon truth, and truth upon fact, what leads to what, what are points primary and what secondary, all this they have yet to learn. It is all a new science to them, and they do not even know their ignorance of it. Moreover, the world of to-day has no connection in their minds with the world of yesterday ; time is not a stream, but stands before them round and full, like the moon. They do not know what happened ten years ago, much less the annals of a century : the past does not live to them in the present ; they do not understand the worth of contested points ; names have no associations for them, and persons kindle no recollections. They hear of men, and things, and projects, and struggles, and principles ; but everything comes and goes like the wind ; nothing makes an impression, nothing penetrates, nothing has its place in their minds. They locate nothing : they have no system. They hear and they forget : or they just recollect what they have once heard, they cannot tell where. Thus they have no consistency in their arguments ; that is, they argue one way to-day, and not exactly the other way to-morrow, but indirectly the other way at random. Their

lines of argument diverge ; nothing comes to a point ; there
is no one centre in which their mind sits, on which their
judgment of men and things proceeds.   This is the state of
many men all through life ; and miserable politicians or Church-
men they make, unless by good luck they are in safe hands,
and ruled by others, or are pledged to a course.   Else they
are at the mercy of the wind and waves ; and without being
Radical, Whig, Tory, or Conservative, High Church or Low
Church, they do Whig acts, Tory acts, Catholic acts, and
Heretical acts, as the fit takes them, or as events or parties
drive them.   And sometimes when their self importance is
hurt, they take refuge in the idea that all this is a proof that
they are unfettered, moderate, dispassionate, that they observe
the mean, that they are no 'party men ;' when they are, in
fact, the most helpless of slaves ; for our strength in this world
is, to be the subjects of the reason and our liberty, to be
captives of the truth."*

How the organization of ideas has fared with higher class
societies others can tell: the working class have been left so
much in want of initiative direction that almost everything has
to be done among them, and an imperfect and brief attempt
to direct those interested in Freethought may meet with some
acceptance.   To clamour for objects without being able to
connect them with principles : to smart under contumely without knowing how to protect themselves : to bear some lofty
name without understanding the manner in which character
should correspond to profession—this is the amount of the
popular attainment.

In this new Edition I find little to alter and less to add.   In
a passage on page 27, the distinction between Secular instruction and Secularism is explained, in these words :—" Secular
education is by some confounded with Secularism, whereas the
distinction between them is very wide.   Secular education
simply means imparting Secular knowledge separately—by
itself, without admixture of Theology with it.   The advocate
of Secular education may be, and generally is, also an
advocate of religion ; but he would teach religion at another
time and treat it as a distinct subject, too sacred for coercive
admixture into the hard and vexatious routine of a school.   He

* " Loss and Gain," ascribed to the Rev. Father Newman.

would confine the inculcation of religion to fitting seasons and chosen instruments. He holds also that one subject at a time is mental economy in learning. Secular education is the policy of a school—Secularism is the policy of life to those who do not accept Theology."

Very few persons admitted that these distinctions existed when this passage was written in 1854. This year, 1870, they have been substantially admitted by the Legislature in concession made in the National Education Bill. It only remains to add that the whole text has been revised and re-arranged in an order which seems more consecutive. The portion on Secular Organizations has been abridged, in part re-written, explaining particulars as to the Secular Guild.

A distinctive summary of Secular principles may be read under the article " Secularism," in Chambers's Cyclopædia.

THE TERM SECULARISM.

CHAPTER II.

" The adoption of the term Secularism is justified by its including a large number of persons who are not Atheists, and uniting them for action which has Secularism for its object, and not Atheism. On this ground, and because, by the adoption of a new term, a vast amount of impediment from prejudice is got rid of, the use of the name Secularism is found advantageous."— HARRIET MARTINEAU. *Boston Liberator.*—Letter to Lloyd Garrison, November, 1853.

EVERY one observant of public controversy in England, is aware of its improved tone of late years. This improved tone is part of a wider progress. Increase of wealth has led to improvement of taste, and the diffusion of knowledge to refinement of sentiment. The mass are better dressed, better mannered, better spoken than formerly. A coffee-room discussion, conducted by mechanics, is now a more decorous exhibition than a debate in Parliament was in the days of Canning * Boisterousness at the tables of the rich, and insolence in the language of the poor, are fast disappear-.ing. "Good society" is now that society in which people practise the art of being genial, without being familiar. and in which an evincible courtesey of speech is no longer regarded as timidity or effeminacy. but rather as proof of a disciplined spirit, which chooses to avoid all offence, the better to maintain the right peremptorily punishing wanton insult. Theologians, more inveterate in speech than politicians, now observe a respectfulness to opponents before unknown. That diversity of opinion once ascribed to "badness of heart" is now, with more discrimination, referred to defect or diversity of under-standing—a change which, discarding invective, recognizes instruction as the agent of uniformity.

Amid all this newness of conception it must be obvious that

---

* From whose lips the House of Commons cheered a reference to a political adversary as " the revered and ruptured Ogden."

many old terms of theological controversy are obsolete. The idea of an "Atheist" as one warring against moral restraints —of an "Infidel" as one treacherous to the truth—of a "Freethinker" as a "loose thinker,"* arose in the darkness of past times, when men fought by the flickering light of their hatreds—times which tradition has peopled with monsters of divinity as well as of nature. But the glaring colours in which the party names invented by past priests were dyed, no longer harmonize with the quieter taste of the present day. The more sober spirit of modern controversy has, therefore, need of new terms, and if the term "Secularism" was merely a neutral substitute for "Freethinking," there would be reason for its adoption. Dissenters might as well continue the designation of "Schismatics," or Political Reformers that of "Anarchists," as that the students of Positive Philosophy should continue the designation "Atheism," "Infidelism," or any similar term by which their opponents have contrived to brand their opinions. It is as though a merchant vessel should consent to carry a pirate flag. Freethinker is, however, getting an acceptable term. Upon the platform, Christian disputants frequently claim it, and resent the exclusive assumption of it by others. These new claimants say, "We are as much Freethinkers as yourselves," so that it is necessary to define Freethinking. It is fearless thinking, based upon impartial inquiry, searching on both sides, not regarding doubt as a crime, or opposite conclusions as a species of moral poison. Those who inquire with sinister pre-possessions will never inquire fairly. The Freethinker fears not to follow a conclusion to the utmost limits of truth, whether it coincides with the Bible or contradicts it. If therefore any pronounce the term "Secularism" "a concealment or a disguise," they can do so legitimately only after detecting some false meaning it is intended to convey, and not on the mere ground of its being a change of name, since nothing can more completely "conceal and disguise" the purposes of Freethought than the old names imposed upon it by its adversaries, which associate with guilt its conscientious conclusions and impute to it as outrages, its acts of self-defence.

Besides the term Secularism, there was another term which seemed to promise also distinctiveness of meaning—namely,

---

* As the Reverend Canon Kingsley has perversely rendered it.

Cosmism, under which adherents would have taken the designation of Cosmists. But this name scientific men would have understood in a purely physical sense, after the great example of Humboldt, and the public would not all have understood it—besides, it was open to easy perversion in one of its declinations. Next to this, as a name, stands that of Realism—intrinsically good. A Society of Realists would have been intelligible, but many would have supposed it to be some revival of the old Realists. Moralism, a sound name in itself, is under Evangelical condemnation as "mere morality." Naturalism would seem an obvious name, were it not that we should be confounded with Naturalists, to say no more. Some name must be taken, as was the case with the Theophilanthropists of Paris. Many of them would rather not have assumed any denomination, but they yielded to the reasonable argument, that if they did not choose one for themselves, the public would bestow upon them one which would be less to their liking. Those who took the name of Philantropes found it exposed them to a pun, which greatly damaged them: *Philantropes* was turned into *filoux en troupe*.

Historical characteristics, however, seemed to point to a term which expressed the Secular element in life: a term deeply engrafted in literature: of irreproachable associations; a term found and respected in the dictionaries of opponents, and to which, therefore, they might dispute our right, but which they could not damage. Instead, therefore, of finding ourselves self-branded or caricatured by this designation, we have found opponents claiming it, and disputing with us for its possession.

PRINCIPLES OF SECULARISM DEFINED.

CHAPTER III.

I.

ECULARISM is the study of promoting human welfare by material means ; measuring human welfare by the utilitarian rule, and making the service of others a duty of life. Secularism relates to the present existence of man, and to action, the issues of which can be tested by the experience of this life— having for its objects the development of the physical, moral, and intellectual nature of man to the highest perceivable point, as the immediate duty of society : inculcating the practical sufficiency of natural morality apart from Atheism, Theism, or Christianity : engaging its adherents in the promotion of human improvement by material means, and making these agreements the ground of common unity for all who would regulate life by reason and ennoble it by service. The Secular is sacred in its influence on life, for by purity of material conditions the loftiest natures are best sustained, and the lower the most surely elevated. Secularism is a series of principles intended for the guidance of those who find Theology indefinite, or inadequate, or deem it unreliable. It replaces theology, which mainly regards life as a sinful necessity, as a scene of tribulation through which we pass to a better world. Secularism rejoices in this life, and regards it as the sphere of those duties which educate men to fitness for any future and better life, should such transpire.

II.

A Secularist guides himself by maxims of Positivism, seeking to discern what *is* in Nature—what *ought* to be in morals—selecting the *affirmative* in exposition, concerning himself with the real, the right, and the constructive. Positive principles are principles which are provable. " A positive precept," says Bishop Butler, "is a precept the reason of which we see." Positivism is policy of material progress.

III.

Science is the available Providence of life. The problem to be solved by a science of Society, is to find that situation in which it shall be impossible for a man to be depraved or poor. Mankind are saved by being served. Spiritual sympathy is a lesser mercy than that forethought which anticipates and extirpates the causes of suffering. Deliverance from sorrow or injustice is before consolation—doing well is higher than meaning well—work is worship to those who accept Theism, and duty to those who do not.

IV.

Sincerity, though not errorless, involves the least chance of error, and is without moral guilt. Sincerity is well-informed, conscientious conviction, arrived at by intelligent examination, animating those who possess that conviction to carry it into practice from a sense of duty. Virtue in relation to opinion consists neither in conformity nor non-conformity, but in sincere beliefs, and in living up to them.

V.

Conscience is higher than Consequence.*

VI.

All pursuit of good objects with pure intent is religiousness in the best sense in which this term appears to be used. A " good object " is an object consistent with truth, honour, justice. love. A pure "intent " is the intent of serving humanity. Immediate service of humanity is not intended to mean instant gratification, but " immediate " in contradistinction to the interest of another life. The distinctive peculiarity of the Secularist is, that he seeks that good which is dictated by Nature, which is attainable by material means, and which is of immediate service to humanity—a religiousness to which the idea of God is not essential, nor the denial of the idea necessary.

---

* Vide Mr. Holdreths' Papers.

VII.

Nearly all inferior natures are susceptible of moral and physical improvability ; this improvability can be indefinitely secured by supplying proper material conditions ; these conditions may one day be supplied by a system of wise and fraternal co-operation, which primarily entrenches itself in common prudence, which enacts service according to industrial capacity, and distributes wealth according to rational needs. Secular principles involve for mankind a future, where there shall exist unity of condition with infinite diversity of intellect, where the subsistence of ignorance and selfishness shall leave men equal, and universal purity enable all things —noble society, the treasures of art, and the riches of the world—to be had in common.

VIII.

Since it is not capable of demonstration whether the inequalties of human condition will be compensated for in another life—it is the business of intelligence to rectify them in this world. The speculative worship of superior beings, who cannot need it, seems a lesser duty than the patient service of known *inferior* natures, and the mitigation of harsh destiny, so that the ignorant may be enlightened and the low elevated.

LAWS OF SECULAR CONTROVERSY.

CHAPTER IV.

I.

RIGHTS of Reason. As a means of developing and establishing Secular principles, and as security that the principles of Nature and the habit of reason may prevail, Secularism uses itself, and maintains for others, as rights of reason:—

The Free Search for Truth, without which its full attainment is impossible.

The Free Utterance of the result, without which the increase of Truth is limited.

The Free Criticism of alleged Truth, without which its identity must remain uncertain.

The Fair Action of Conviction thus attained, without which conscience will be impotent on practice.

II.

Standard of Appeal. "Secularism accepts no authority but that of Nature, adopts no methods but those of science and philosophy, and respects in practice no rule but that of the conscience, illustrated by the common sense of mankind. It values the lessons of the past, and looks to tradition as presenting a storehouse of raw materials to thought, and in many cases results of high wisdom for our reverence: but it utterly disowns tradition as a ground of belief, whether miracles and supernaturalism be claimed or not claimed on its side. No sacred scripture or ancient church can be made a basis of belief, for the obvious reason that their claims always need to be proved, and cannot-without absurdity be assumed. The association leaves to its individual members to yield whatever respect their own good sense judges to be due to the opinions of great men, living or dead, spoken or written, as also to the practice of ancient communities, national or ecclesiastical. But it disowns all appeal to such authorities as final tests of truth."*

III.

Sphere of Controversy. Since the principles of Secularism rest on grounds apart from Theism, Atheism, or Christianity, it is not logically necessary for Secularists to debate the truth of these subjects. In controversy, Secularism concerns itself with the assertion and maintenance of its own affirmative propositions, combating only views of Theology and Christianity so far as they interfere with, discourage, or disparage Secular action, which may be done without digressing into the discussion of the truth of Theism or divine origin of the Bible.

IV.

Personal Controversy. A Secularist will avoid indiscriminate disparagement of bodies or antagonism of persons, and will place before himself simply the instruction and service of an opponent, whose sincerity he will not question, whose motives he will not impugn, always holding that a man whom it is not worth while confuting courteously, is not worth while confuting at all. Such disparagements as are included in the explicit condemnation of erroneous principles are, we believe, all that the public defence of opinion requires, and are the only kind of disparagement a Secularist proposes to employ.

V.

Justification of Controversy. The universal fair and open discussion of opinion is the highest guarantee of public truth—only that theory which is submitted to that ordeal is to be regarded, since only that which endures it can be trusted. Secularism encourages men to trust reason throughout, and to trust nothing that reason does not establish—to examine all things hopeful, respect all things probable, but rely upon nothing without precaution which does not come within the range of science and experience.

* "Programme of Freethought Societies," by F. W. Newman. (REASONER, No. 388.)

MAXIMS OF ASSOCIATION.

CHAPTER V.

I.

IT is the duty of every man to regulate his personal and family interests so as to admit of some exertions for the improvement of society. It is only by serving those beyond ourselves that we can secure for ourselves protection, sympathy, or honour. The neglect of home for public affairs endangers philanthropy, by making it the enemy of the household. To suffer, on the other hand, the interests of the family to degenerate into mere selfism, is a dangerous example to rulers.

II.

"No man or woman is accountable to others for any conduct by which others are not injured or damaged."*

III.

Social freedom consists in being subject to just rule and to none other.

IV.

Service and endurance are the chief personal duties of man.

V.

Secularism holds it to be the duty of every man to reserve a portion of his means and energies for the public service, and so to cultivate and cherish his powers, mental and physical, as

---

* D. in the LEADER, 1850, who, as a correspondent, first expressed this aphorism thus.

to have them ever ready to perform service, as efficient as possible, to the well-being of humanity. No weakness, no passion, no wavering, should be found among those who are battling for the cause of human welfare, which such errors may fatally injure. Self-control, self-culture, self-sacrifice, are all essential to those who would serve that cause, and would not bring discredit upon their comrades in that service.*

VI.

To promote in good faith and good temper the immediate and material welfare of humanity, in accordance with the laws of Nature, is the study and duty of a Secularist, and this is the unity of principle which prevails amid whatever diversity of opinion may subsist in a Secular Society, the bond of union being the common convictions of the duty of advancing the Secular good of this life, of the authority of natural morality, and of the utility of material effort in the work of human improvement. In other words, Secularist union implies the concerted action of all who believe it right to promote the Secular good of this life, to teach morality, founded upon the laws of Nature, and to seek human improvement by material methods, irrespective of any other opinions held, and irrespective of any diversity of reasons for holding these.

* Mr. L. H. Holdreth, Religion of Duty.

THE SECULAR GUILD.

CHAPTER VI.

SEVERAL expositors of Secular principles, able to act together, have for many years endeavoured by counsel, by aid and by publication to promote Secular organization. At one time they conducted a Secular Institute in Fleet Street, London—in 1854. The object was to form Secular Societies for teaching the positive results of Freethought. In the first edition of this work it was held to be desirable that there should be a centre of reference for all inquirers upon Secular principles at home and abroad. Attention should be guaranteed to distant correspondents and visitors, so that means of communication and publication of all advanced opinions in sociology, theology, and politics might exist, and be able to command publicity, when expressed dispassionately, impersonally, and with ordinary good taste.

It has been generally admitted that the operations at that time conducted, helped to impart a new character to Freethought advocacy, and many of its recommendations have since been copied by associations subsequently formed. The promoters of Secularism alluded to, have not ceased in the *Reasoner* and other publications, by lectures, by statements, by articles, by pamphlets to urge a definite and consistent representation of Secular and Freethought principles: as many mistake merely mechanical association for the organization of ideas.

The promoters in question have since adopted the form of action of a Secular Guild, and continue the *Reasoner* (of which there is now issued a " Review Series ") as their organ. The objects of a Council of the Guild is to promote, as far as means may permit, or counsel prevail, organization of ideas :—

1.—To train Advocates of Secular principles.

2.—To advise an impersonal policy of advocacy, which seeking to carry its ends by force of exposition, rather than of denunciation, shall command the attention and respect of those who influence public affairs.

3.—To promote solution of political, social, and educational questions on Secular and unsectarian grounds.*

4.—To point out new Books of Secular relevance, and where possible, to accredit Advocates of Secularism that the public may have some guidance, and the party be no longer liable to be judged by whoever may appear to write or speak on the subject.

5.—To assist in the protection and defence of those injured, or attempted to be injured on account of Freethought or Secularist opinion.

6.—To provide for the administration of property bequeathed for Secular purposes, of which so much has been lost through the injustice of the law, and machinations of persons opposed to Liberal views.

7.—When a member has been honourably counted on the side of Secularism, has been a Subscriber or a Worker for a term of years, the Guild, keeping a record of such Service, proposes to give a Certificate of it which among Friends of Freethought may be a passport to recognition and esteem. To constitute some such Freemasonry in Freethought, may elevate association in England. A certificate of Illuminism or of Carbonarism in Italy was once handed down from father to son as an heirloom of honour, while in England you have to supplicate men to join a society of progression, instead of membership being a distinction which men shall covet. At present a man who has given the best years of his life to the public service is liable (if from any necessity he ceases to act) to be counted a renegade by men who have never rendered twelve months' consecutive or costly service themselves. There ought to be a fixed term of Service, which, if honourably and effectively rendered, should entitle a man to be considered free, as a soldier after leaving the army, and his certificate of having belonged to the Order of Secularism should entitle him to distinction and to authority when his opinion was sought, and to exemption from all but voluntary service. At present the soldiers of Progress, when no longer able to serve, are dismissed from the public eye, like the race-horse to the cab stand, to obscurity and neglect. This needs correction before men can be counted upon in the battle of Truth. A man is to be estimated according to the aims of the party to which he is allied. He is to be esteemed in consequence of sacrifices of time, and discipline of conduct, which he contributes to the service and reputation of his cause.

In foreign countries many persons reside interested in Secularism; in Great Britain indeed many friends reside where

---

* This has been done to some extent in the discussion of the National Education question. The Proposer of the Guild contributed what he could to this end by reading the paper published in the proceedings of the Conference of the Birmingham Education League, by letters like that to the *Daily News*, commented upon by the Bishop of Peterborough, at Leicester [see official publications of the Manchester National Education Union,] by discussions as those with the Revs. Pringle and Baldwin, at Norwich, and with Mr. Chas. Bradlaugh, at the Old Street Hall of Science, London ; and by Lectures during the time the question of National Education has been before Parliament.

no Secular Society is formed ; and in these cases membership of the Guild would be advantageous to them, affording means of introduction to publicists of similar views : and even in instances of towns where Secular Societies do exist, persons in direct relation to the Secular Guild would be able to furnish Secular direction where the tradition and usage of a Secular Society are unknown, or unfamiliar.

ORGANIZATION INDICATED.

CHAPTER VII.

A S the aim of the Guild is not to fetter independent thought, but to concert practical action, it is mainly required of each member that he undertakes to perform, in good faith, the duties which he shall consent to have assigned to him; and generally so to comport himself that his principles shall not be likely to suffer, if judged by his conduct. He will be expected to treat every colleague as equal with himself in veracity, in honour, and in loyalty to his cause. And every form of speech which casts a doubt upon the truth, or imputes, or assumes a want of honour on the part of any member, will be deemed a breach of order. If any member intends such an accusation of another, it must be made the matter of a formal charge, after leave obtained to prefer it.

What it is desirable to know about new members is this: —

Do they, in their conception of Secularism, see in it that which seeks not the sensual but the good, and a good which the conscience can be engaged in pursuing and promoting; a Moralism in accordance with the laws of Nature and capable of intrinsic proof: a Materialism which is definite without dogmatism or grossness; and a unity on the ground of these common agreements, for convictions which imply no apostolate are neither earnest nor generous. No one ought to be encouraged to take sides with Secularism, unless his conscience is satisfied of the moral rightfulness of its principles and duties both for life and death.

It is not desirable to accept persons of that class who decry parties—who boast of being of no party—who preach up isolation, and lament the want of unity—who think party the madness of the many, for the gain of the few. Seek rather the partisan who is wise enough to know that the disparagement of party is the madness of the few, leading to the utter impotence of the many. A party, in an associative and defensible sense, is a class of persons taking sides upon some definite question, and acting together for necessary ends, having principles, aims, policy, authority, and discipline.*

With respect to proposed members, it may be well to ascertain whether neglect, or rudeness, or insult, or unfairness from colleagues, or overwork being imposed upon him, or incapacity of others, would divert him from his duty. These accidents or necessities might occur : but if a society is to be strong it must be able to count upon its members, and to be able to count upon them it must be known what they will bear without insubordination; and what they will bear will depend upon the frankness and completeness of information they receive as to the social risks all run who unite to carry out any course of duty or public service.

Always assuming that a candidate cares for the objects for which he proposes to associate, and that it is worth while knowing whom it is with whom you propose to work them out ; answers to such inquiries as the following would tend to impart a working knowledge and quality to the society :—

Is he a person previously or recently acquainted with the principles he is about to profess ?

Does he understand what is meant by "taking sides " with a public party ? Would he be faithful to the special ideas of Secularism so long as he felt them to be true ? Would he make sacrifices to spread them and vindicate them, or enable others to do so ? Would he conceive of Secularism as a cause to be served loyally, which he would support as well as he was able, if unable to support it as well as he could wish ?

Is he of decent, moral character, and tolerably reliable as to his future conduct ?

In presenting his views to others, would he be likely to render them in an attractive spirit, or to make them disagreeable to others ?

Is he of an impulsive nature, ardent for a time, and then apathetic or reactionary—likely to antagonize to-morrow the persons he applauds to-day ?

Is he a person who would commit the fault of provoking persecution ? Would ridicule or persecution chill him if it occurred ? Is he a man to stand by an obscure and friendless cause—or are notoriety, success, applause, and the company of others, indispensable to his fidelity ?

Is he a man of any mark of esteem among his friends—a man whose promise is sure, whose word has weight ?

Is his idea of obedience, obedience simply to his own will ? Would he acquiesce in the authority of the laws of the Society, or the decision of the Society where the laws were silent ? Would he acknowledge in democracy the despotism of principles self-consented to—or as an arena for the

* In a school there is usually teaching, training, discipline, science, system, authorities, tradition, and development.—TIMES, 1846.

assertion of Individualism before winning the consent of colleagues to the discussion of special views?

The membership sought may be granted, provided the actual knowledge of Secular principles be satisfactory, and evident earnestness to practise them be apparent. The purport of the whole of the questions is to enable ·a clear opinion to be formed as to what is to be expected of the new member—how far he is likely to be reliable—how long he is likely to remain with us—under what circumstances he is likely to fail us—what work may be assigned him—what confidences he may be entrusted with, and in what terms he should be introduced to colleagues, and spoken of to others.

The Membership here described would and should be no restricted and exclusive society, where only one pattern of efficiency prevails; but a society where all diversities of capacity, energy, and worth, may be found, so far as it is honest and trustworthy. A Society, like the State, requires the existence of the people, as well as public officers—men who can act, as well as men who can think and direct. Many men who lack refinement, and even discretion, possess courage and energy, and will go out on the inevitable "forlorn hopes" of progress; which the merely prudent avoid, and from which the cultivated too often shrink. Our work requires all orders of men, but efficiency requires that we know which is which, that none may be employed in the dark.

In every public organization there are persons who promote and aid unconnected with the Society.

Active members are those who engage to perform specific duties; such as reporting lectures, sermons, and public meetings, so far as they refer to Secularism.*

To give notice of meetings and sermons about to be held or delivered for or against Secularism.

To note and report passages in books, newspapers, magazines, and reviews referring to Secularism.

Each active member should possess some working efficiency, or be willing to acquire it. To be able to explain his views by tongue or pen with simple directness, to observe carefully,

---

* In reporting, each member should be careful to understate rather than overstate facts, distinguishing carefully what is matter of knowledge from rumour, conjecture, or opinion.

to report judiciously, to reason dispassionately, to put the best construction on every act that needs interpretation, are desirable accomplishments in a Propagandist.

In all public proceedings of the Society, written speeches should be preferred from the young, because such speeches admit of preconsidered brevity, consecutiveness, and purpose. and exist for reference. In the deliberations and discussions of any Society, it might usefully be deemed a qualification to make a contribution to the subject in speeches brief and direct.

Non-reliableness in discharge of duties, or moral disqualification, shall be a ground of annulling membership, which may be done after the member objected to has had a fair opportunity of defending himself from the specific disqualifications alleged against him and communicated to him, and has failed therein.

The duties assigned to each member should be such as are within his means, as respects power and opportunity; such, indeed, as interfere neither with his social nor civil obligations: the intention being that the membership of the Society shall not as a rule be incompatible with the preservation of health, and the primary service due to family and the State.*

Any persons acquainted with the "Principles of Secularism" here given, who shall generally agree therein, and associate under any name to promote such objects, and to act in concert with all who seek similar objects, and will receive and take into official consideration the instructions of the Guild, and to make one subscription yearly among its members and friends on behalf of its Propagandist Funds, shall be recognized as a Branch of it.

---

* As a general rule, it will be found that any one who sacrifices more than one-fifth of his time and means will become before long reactionary, and not only do nothing himself, but discourage others.

THE PLACE OF SECULARISM.

CHAPTER VIII.

" We do not, however, deny that, false as the whole theory [of Secularism] appears to us, it is capable of attracting the belief of large numbers of people, and of exercising considerable influence over their conduct ; and we should admit that the influence so exercised is considerably better than no influence at all."—*Saturday Review*, July 2, 1859.

THIS first step is to win, from public opinion, a standing place for Secularism. So long as people believe Secularism not to be wanted, indeed impossible to be wanted—that it is error, wickedness, and unmitigated evil, it will receive no attention, no respect, and make no way. But show that it occupies a vacant place, supplies a want, is a direction where no other party supplies any—and it at once appears indispensable. It is proved to be a service to somebody, and from that moment it is tolerated if not respected. It may be like war, or medicine, or work, or law, disagreeable or unpalatable, but when seen to be necessary, it will have recognition and support. We are sure this case can be made out for Secularism. It is not only true, but it is known ; it is not only known, but it is notorious, that there are thousands and tens of thousands of persons in every district of this and most European countries, who are without the pale of Christianity. They reject it, they disprove it, they dislike it, or they do not understand it. Some have vices and passions which Christianity, as preached around them, condemns. As Devils are said to do, they "believe and tremble," and so disown what they have not the virtue to practise. Faith does not touch them, and reason is not tried—indeed reason is decried by the evangelically religious, so that not being converted in one way, no other way is open to them. Others are absorbed or insensate ; they are busy, or stupid, or defiant, and regard Christianity as a waste of time, or as monotonous or offensive. It bores them or threatens them. They are already dull, therefore it does not attract them— they have some rude sense of independence and some feeling of courage, and they object either to be snubbed into conformity or kicked into heaven. Another and a yearly increasing portion of the people have, after patiently and

painfully thinking over Christianity, come to believe it to be
untrue ; unfounded historically ; wrong morally, and a dis-
creditable imputation upon God. It outrages their affections,
it baffles their understandings. It is double tongued. Its
expounders are always multiplying, and the more they increase
the less they agree, and hence sceptics the more abound.
Disbelievers therefore exist ; they augment : they can neither
be convinced, converted, nor conciliated, because they will yield
no allegiance to a system which has no hold on their conscience.
It is, we repeat, more than known, it is notorious that these
persons live and die in scepticism. These facts are the cry of
the pulpit, the theme of the platform, the burden of the
religious tract. Now, is nothing to be done with these people ?
You cannot exterminate them, the Church cannot direct them.
The Bible is no authority to them—the " will of God," as the
clergy call it, in their eyes is mere arbitrary, capricious, dog-
matical assumption ; sometimes, indeed, wise precept, but
oftener a cloak for knavery or a pretext for despotism. To
open the eyes of such persons to the omnipresent teachings of
Nature, to make reason an authority with them, to inspire them
with precepts which experience can verify—to connect conscience with intelligence, right with interest, duty with self-
respect, and goodness with love, must surely be useful.   If
Secularism accomplishes some such work, where Christianity
confessedly accomplishes nothing, it certainly has a place of
its own. It is no answer to it to claim that Christianity is higher,
more complete, better. The advocates of every old religion, say
the same. Christianity may be higher, more complete, better
—for somebody else.   But nothing can be high, complete, or
good, for those who do not see it, accept it, want it, or act
upon it.   That is first which is fit—that is supreme which is
most productive of practical virtue. No comparison (which
would be as irrelevant as offensive) between Secularism and
Christianity is set up here. The question is—is Secularism
useful, or may it be useful to anybody ? The question is not—
does it contain *all* truth ? but does it contain as much as may
be serviceable to many minds, otherwise uninfluenced for good ?
Arithmetic is useful though Algebra is more compendious.
Mensuration performs good offices in hands ignorant of Euclid.
There may be logic without Whately, and melody without
Beethoven ; and there may be Secular ethics which shall be
useful without the pretension of Christianity.

CHARACTERISTICS OF SECULARISM.

CHAPTER IX.

I.

SECULARISM means the moral duty of man in this life deduced from considerations which pertain to this life alone. Secular education is by some confounded with Secularism, whereas the distinction between them is very wide. Secular education simply means imparting Secular knowledge separately—by itself, without admixture of Theology with it. The advocate of Secular education may be, and generally is, also an advocate of religion; but he would teach religion at another time and treat it as a distinct subject, too sacred for coercive admixture into the hard and vexatious routine of a school. He would confine the inculcation of religion to fitting seasons and chosen instruments. He holds also that one subject at a time is mental economy in learning. Secular education is the policy of a school—Secularism is a policy of life to those who do not accept Theology. Secularity draws the line of separation between the things of time and the things of eternity. That is Secular which pertains to this world. The distinction may be seen in the fact that the cardinal propositions of Theology are provable only in the next life, and not in this. If I believe in a given creed it may turn out to be the true one; but one must die to find that out. On this side of the grave all is doubt; the truth of Biblical creeds is an affair of hope and anxiety, while the truth of things Secular becomes apparent in time. The advantages arising from the practice of veracity, justice, and temperance can be ascertained from human experience. If we are told to "fear God and keep His commandments," lest His judgments overtake us, the indirect action of this doctrine on human character may make a vicious timid man better in this life, supposing the interpretation of the will of God, and the commandments selected to be enforced, are moral; but such teaching is not Secular, because its main object is to fit men for eternity. Pure Secular principles have for their object to fit men for time, making the fulfilment of human duty here the standard of fitness for any accruing future. *Secularism purposes to regulate human affairs by considerations purely human.* Its principles are founded upon Nature, and its object is to render man as perfect as possible in this life. Its problem is this: Supposing no other life to be before us, what is the wisest use of this? As the Rev. Thomas Binney puts it, " I believe * * that even * * if there were really no God over him, no heaven above, or eternity in prospect, things are so constituted that man may turn the materials of his little life poem, if not always into a grand epic, mostly into something of interest and beauty ; and it is worth his while doing so, even if there should be no sequel to the piece."* Chalmers, Archbishop Whately, and earlier distinguished divines of the Church of England, the most con- spicuous of whom is Bishop Butler, have admitted the independent existence of morality, but we here cite Mr. Binney's words because among Dissenters this truth is less readily admitted. A true Secular life does not exclude any from supplementary speculations. Not until we have fulfilled our duty to man, as far as we can ascertain that duty, can we consistently pretend to comprehend the more difficult relations of man to God. Our duties to humanity, understood and dis- charged to the best of our ability, will in no way unfit us to " reverently meditate on things far beyond us, on Power un- limited, on space unfathomed, on time uncounted, on ' whence ' we came, and ' whither ' we go."† The leading ideas of Secularism are humanism, moralism, materialism, utilitarian unity: Humanism, the physical perfection of this life—Moralism, founded on the laws of Nature, as the guid- ance of this life—Materialism, as the means of Nature for the Secular improvement of this life—Unity of thought and action upon these practical grounds. Secularism teaches that the good of the present life is the immediate concern of man, and that it should be his first endeavour to raise it. Secularism inculcates a Morality founded independently upon the laws of Nature. It seeks human improvement through purity and suit- ableness of material conditions as being a method at once moral, practical, universal, and sure.

---

* " How to make the best of both worlds," p. 11.
† F. W. Newman.

II.

The province of Positivism is not speculation upon the origin, but study of the laws of Nature—its policy is to destroy error by superseding it. Auguste Comte quotes, as a cardinal maxim of scientific progress, the words "nothing is destroyed until it is replaced," a proverbial form of a wise saying of M. Necker that in political progress "nothing is destroyed for which we do not find a substitute." Negations, useful in their place, are iconoclastic—not constructive. Unless substitution succeeds destruction—there can be no sustained progress. The Secularist is known by setting up and maintaining affirmative propositions. He replaces negations by affirmations, and substitutes demonstration for denunciation. He asserts truths of Nature and humanity, and reverses the position of the priest who appears as the sceptic, the denier, the disbeliever in Nature and humanity. Statesmen, not otherwise eager for improvement, will regard affirmative proposals. Lord Palmerston could say—"Show me a good and I will realize it—not an abuse to correct."

III.

"All science," says M. Comte, "has prevision for its end, an axiom which separates science from erudition, which relates to events of the past without any regard to the future. No accumulation of facts can effect prevision until the facts are made the basis of reasonings. A knowledge of phenomena leads to prevision, and prevision to action;" or, in other words, when we can foresee what will happen under given circumstances, we can provide against it. It by no means follows that every Secularist will be scientific, but to discern the value of science, to appreciate and promote it, may be possible to most. Science requires high qualities of accurate observation, close attention, careful experiment, caution, patience, labour. Its value to mankind is inestimable. One physician will do more to alleviate human suffering than ten priests. One physical discovery will do more to advance civilization than a generation of prayer-makers. "To get acquaintance with the usual course of Nature (which Science alone can teach us), is a kind of knowledge which pays very good interest."* The value of this knowledge becomes more apparent the longer we live. There

---

* Athenæum, No. 1,637, March 12, 1859.

may be a general superintending Providence—there may be
a Special Providence, but the first does not interfere in human
affairs, and the interpositions of the second are no longer to
be counted upon. The age of Prayer for temporal deliverance has confessedly passed away. But without disputing
these points, it is clear that the only help *available* to man,
the sole dependence upon which he can *calculate*, is that of
Science. Nothing can be more impotent than the fate of that
man who seeks social elevation by mere Faith. All human
affairs are a process, and he alone who acts upon this knowledge can hope to control results. Loyola foresaw the necessity of men acting for human purposes, as though there were
no God. " Let us pray," said he, " as if we had no help in ourselves: *let us labour as if there was no help for us in heaven.*"
Society is a blunder, not a science, until it ensures good sense
and competence for the many. Why this process is tardy,
is that creedists get credit for hoping and meaning well.
Creedists of good intent, who make no improvement and
attempt none, are very much in the way of human betterance.
The spiritualist regards the world theoretically as a gross
element, which he is rather to struggle against than to work
with. This makes human service a mortification instead of
pure passion. We would not deify the world, that is, set up
the sensualism of the body, as spiritualism is set up as the
sensualism of the soul. Secularism seeks the material purity
of the present life, which is at once the *means* and *end* of Secular
endeavour. The most reliable means of progress is the *improvement of material condition*, and " purity " implies " improvement," for there can be no improvement without it. The aim
of all improvement is higher purity. All power, art, civilization and progress are summed up in the result—purer life.
Strength, intellect, love are measured by it. Duty, study,
temperance, patience are but ministers to this. " There is that,"
says Ruskin, " to be seen in every street and lane of every city,
that to be found and felt in every human heart and countenance,
that to be loved in every road-side weed and moss-grown wall,
which, in the hands of faithful men, may convey emotions
of glory and sublimity continual and exalted."

IV.

It is necessary to point out that Sincerity does not imply infallibility. " There is a truth, which could it be stamped

on every human mind, would exterminate all bigotry and persecution. I mean the truth, that worth of character and true integrity, and, consequently, God's acceptance, are not necessarily connected with any particular set of opinions."* If you admit that Mark and Paul were honest, most Christians take that to be an admission of the truth of all related under their names. Yet if a man in defending his opinions, affirm his own sincerity, Christians quickly see that is no proof of their truth, and proceed to disprove them. Sincerity may account for a man holding his opinions, but it does not account for the opinions themselves. Nothing is more common than uninformed, misinformed, mistaken, or self-deluded honesty. But sincere error, though dangerous enough, has not the attribute of crime about it—personal intention of mischief. "Because human nature is frail and fallible, the ground of our acceptance with God, under the Gospel, is *sincerity*. A sincere desire to know and do the will of God, is the only condition of obtaining the Christian salvation. Every honest man will be saved."† But Sincerity, if the reader recurs to our definition of it, includes a short intellectual and moral education with respect to it. Those worthy of the high descriptive "sincere," are those who have thought, inquired, examined, are in earnest, have a sense of duty with regard to their conviction, which is only satisfied by acting upon it. These processes may not bring a man to the truth, but they bring him near to it. The chances of error are reduced hereby as far as human care can reduce them. Secularism holds that the Protestant right of private judgment includes the moral innocency of that judgment, when conscientiously formed, whether for or against received opinion; that though *all sincere opinion is not equally true, nor equally useful, it is yet equally without sin;* that it is not sameness of belief but sincerity of belief which justifies conduct, whether regard be had to the esteem of men or the approval of God. Sincerity, we repeat, is not infallibility. The conscientious are often as mischievous as the false, but he who acts according to the best of his belief is free from criminal intention. The sincerity commended by the Secularist is an active sentiment seeking the truth and acting upon it—not the

---

* Dr. Price.
† John Foster's Tracts on Heresy.

fortuitous, insipid, apathetic, inherited consent, which so often passes for honesty, because too indolent or too cowardly to inquire, and too stupid to doubt. The man who holds merely ready-made opinions is not to be placed on the same level with him whose convictions are derived from experience. True sincerity is an educated and earnest sentiment.

V.

In the formation and judgment of opinions we must take into account the consequences to mankind involved in their adoption. But when an opinion seems true in itself and beneficial to society, the consequences in the way of inconvenience to ourselves is not sufficient reason for refusing to act upon it. If a particular time of enforcing it seem to be one when it will be disregarded, or misunderstood, or put back, and the sacrifice of ourselves on its behalf produce no adequate advantage to society, it may be lawful to seek a better opportunity. We must, however, take care that this view of the matter is not made a pretext of cowardice or evasion of duty. And in no case is it justifiable to belie conscience or profess a belief the contrary of that which we believe to be true. There may in extreme cases be neutrality with regard to truth, but in no case should there be complicity in falsehood. So much with respect to this life. With respect to Deity or another life, we may in all cases rely upon this, that in truth alone is safety. With God, conscience can have no penal consequences. Conscience is the voice of honesty, and honesty, with all its errors, a God of Truth will regard. "We have," says Blanco White, "no revealed rule which will ascertain, with moral certainty, which doctrines are right and which are wrong—that is, as they are known to God." * * "Salvation, therefore, cannot depend on orthodoxy; it cannot consist in abstract doctrines, about which men of equal abilities, virtue, and sincerity are, and always have been, divided." * * "No error on abstract doctrines can be heresy, in the sense of a wrong belief which endangers the soul." "The Father of the Universe accommodates not His judgments to the wretched wranglings of pedantic theologians, but every one who seeks truth, *whether he findeth it or not*, and worketh righteousness, will be accepted of Him."* Thomas

---

* Bishop Watson's Theological Tracts. Introductory.

Carlyle was the first English writer, having the ear of the public, who declared in England that "sincere *doubt* is as much
entitled to respect as sincere *belief*."

VI.

Going to a distant town to mitigate some calamity there, will
illustrate the principle of action prescribed by Secularism.
One man will go on this errand from pure sympathy with
the unfortunate ; this is goodness. Another goes because his
priest bids him ; this is obedience. Another goes because the
twenty-fifth chapter of Matthew tells him that all such persons will pass to the right hand of the Father ; this is calculation. Another goes because he believes God commands him ;
this is piety. Another goes because he believes that the
neglect of suffering will not answer ; this is utilitarianism.
But another goes on the errand of mercy, because it is an
errand of mercy, because it is an immediate service to humanity ; and he goes to attempt material amelioration rather than
spiritual consolation ; this is Secularism, which teaches that
goodness is sanctity, that Nature is guidance, that reason is
authority, that service is duty, and that Materialism is help.

VII.

The policy of Secular controversy is to distinguish and
assert its own affirmative propositions. It is the policy of Secularism not so much to say to error "It is false," as to say of
truth " This is true." Thus, instead of leaving to the popular
theology the prestige of exclusive affirmation accorded to it
by the world, although it is solely employed in the incessant
re-assertion of error, Secularism causes it to own and publish
its denial of positive principle ; when the popular theology
proves itself to be but an organized negation of the moral
guidance of nature and its tendencies to progress. A Secularist sees clearly upon what he relies as a Secularist. To
him the teaching of Nature is as clear as the teaching of the
Bible : and since, if God exists, Nature is certainly His work,
while it is not so clear that the Bible is—the teaching of Nature
will be preferred and followed where the teaching of the Bible
appears to conflict with it. A Secular Society, contemplating
intellectual and moral progress, must provide for the freest
expression of opinion on all subjects which its members may
deem conducive to their common objects. Christianism, Theism,

c

Materialism, and Atheism will be regarded as open questions, subject to unreserved discussion.   But these occasions will be the opportunity of the members, not the business of the society. All public proceedings accredited by the society should relate to topics consistent with the common principles of Secularism. "In necessary things, unity : in doubtful things, liberty : in all things, charity."*   The destruction of religious servitude may be attempted in two ways.   It may be denounced, which will irritate it, or it may be superseded by the servitude of humanity. Attacking it by denunciation, generally inflames and precipitates the persecution of the many upon the few ; when the weak are liable to be scattered, the cowardly to recant, and the brave to perish.

VIII.

The essential rule upon which personal association can be permanent, or controversy be maintained in the spirit in which truth can be evolved, is that of never imputing evil motives nor putting the worst construction on any act.   Free Inquiry has no limits but truth. Free Speech no limits but exactness, Policy (here the law of speech) no limits but usefulness. Unfettered and uncompromising are they who pursue free inquiry throughout—measured and impassable may those become, who hold to a generous veracity. Far both from outrage or servility—too proud to court and too strong to hate—are those who learn to discard all arts but that of the austere service of others, exacting no thanks and pausing at no curse.   Wise words of counsel to Theological controversialists have been addressed in a powerful quarter of public opinion : " Religious controversy has already lost much of its bitterness. Open abuse and exchange of foul names are exploded, and even the indirect imputation of unworthy motives is falling into disuse.   Another step will be made when theologians have learnt to extend their intellectual as well as their moral sympathies, to feel that most truths are double edged. and not to wage an unnecessary war against opinion which. strange, incongruous, and unlovely as they may at first appear, are built, perhaps, on as firm a foundation, and are held with equal sincerity and good faith, as their own."+   This is advice which both sides should remember.

* Maxim (much unused) of the Roman Catholic Church.
† TIMES Leader of November 8, 1855.

IX.

"No society can be in a healthy state in which eccentricity is a matter of reproach." Conventionality is the tyranny of the average man, and a despicable tyranny it is. The tyranny of genius is hard to be borne—that of mediocrity is humiliating. That idea of freedom which consists in the absence of all government is either mere lawlessness, or refers to the distant period when each man having attained perfection will be a law unto himself. Just rule is indispensable rule, and none other. The fewer laws consistent with the public preservation the better—there is, then, as Mr. Mill has shown in his "Liberty," the more room for that ever-recurring originality which keeps intellect alive in the world. Towards law kept within the limits of reason, obedience is the first of virtues. "Order and Progress," says Comte, which we should express thus:—Order, without which Progress is impossible: Progress, without which Order, is Tyranny. The world is clogged with men of dead principles. Principles that cannot be acted upon are probably either obsolete or false. One certain way to improvement is to exact consistency between profession and practice ; and the way to bring this about is to teach that the highest merit consists in having earnest views and in endeavouring to realize them—and this whether the convictions be contained within or without accredited creeds. There will be no progress except within the stereotyped limits of creeds, unless means are found to justify independent convictions to the conscience. To the philosopher you have merely to show that a thing is true, to the statesman, that it is useful, but to a Christian, that it is safe. The grace of service lies in its patience. To promote the welfare of others, irrespective of their gratitude or claims, is to reach the nature of the Gods. It is a higher sentiment than is ascribed to the Deity of the Bible. The abiding disposition to serve others is the end of all philosophy. The vow of principle is always one of poverty and obedience, and few are they who take it—and fewer who keep it. If hate obscure for a period the path of duty, let us remember nothing should shake our attachment to that supreme thought, which at once stills human anger and educates human endeavour—the perception that "the sufferings and errors of mankind arise out of want of knowledge rather than defect of goodness."

X.

A leading object of Secularism is the promotion of the
material purity of the present life—" material purity," which
includes personal as well as external condition.   The question
of Spiritualism (without employing it and without disparaging
it) it regards as a distinct question, and hence the methods
by which Secularists attempt "improvement" will be "material"
as being the most reliable.   The tacit or expressed aim of all
Freethinking, has ever been true thinking and pure thinking.
It has been a continued protest against the errors Theology
has introduced, and the vicious relations it has conserved and
sanctified.   It is necessary to mark this, and it can be done by
insisting and keeping distinctly evident that the aim of Secularism is the purity of material influences.   This precludes the
possibility of Secularism being charged either with conscious
grossness or intentional sin.   Secularism concerns itself with
the work of to-day.   " It is always yesterday or to-morrow,
and never to-day,"* is a fair description of life according to
theologies.   Secularism, on the contrary, concerns itself with
the things of " to-day."

> To know
> That which before us lies in daily life
> Is the prime wisdom.

The cardinal idea of the " popular Theology " is the necessity of Revelation.   It believes that the light of Nature is
darkness, that Reason affords no guidance, that the Scriptures
are the true chart, the sole chart, and the sufficient chart of
man, and it regards all attempts to delineate a chart of
Nature as impious, as impracticable, and as a covert attack
upon the Biblical chart in possession of the churches.   Knowing no other guidance than that of the Bible, and disbelieving
the possibility of any other, theology denounces Doubt, which
inspires it with a sense of insecurity—it fears Inquiry, which
may invalidate its trust—and deprecates Criticism, which may
expose it, if deficient.   Having nothing to gain, it is reluctant
to incur risk—having all to lose, it dreads to be disturbed—
having no strength but in Faith, it fears those who Reason—
and less from ill-will than from the tenderness of its position,
it persecutes in self-defence.   Such are the restrictions and the
logic of Theology.

---

* Story of Boots, by Dickens.

XI.

On the other hand, Rationalism (which is the logic of Nature) is in attitude and spirit quite the reverse. It observes that numbers are unconvinced of the fact of Revelation, and feel the insufficiency, for their guidance, of that offered to them. To them the pages of Nature seem clearer than those of the Apostles. Reason, which existed before all Religions and decides upon all—else the false can never be distinguished from the true—seems self-dependent and capable of furnishing personal direction. Hence Rationalism instructed by facts, winning secrets by experiments, establishing principles by reflection, is assured of a morality founded upon the laws of Nature. Without the advantage of inductive science to assist discoveries, or the printing press to record corroborations of them, the Pre-Christian world created ethics, and Socrates. and Epictetus, and Zoroaster and Confucius, delivered precepts, to which this age accords a high place. Modern Rationalists therefore sought, with their new advantages, to augment and systematize these conquests. They tested the claims of the Church by the truths of Nature. That Freethought which had won these truths applied them to creeds, and criticism became its weapon of Propagandism. Its consciousness of new truth stimulated its aggression on old error. The pretensions of reason being denied as false, and rationalists themselves persecuted as dangerous, they had no alternative but to criticise in order to vindicate their own principles, and weaken the credit and power of their opponents. To attack the misleading dogmas of Theology was to the early Freethinkers well understood self-defence. In some hands and under the provocations of vindictive bigotry, this work, no doubt, became wholly antagonistic, but the main aspiration of the majority was the determination of teaching the people "to be a law unto themselves." They found prevailing a religion of unreasoning faith. They sought to create a religion of intelligent conviction, whose uniformity consisted in sincerity. Its believers did not all hold the same tenets, but they all sought the same truth and pursued it with the same earnestness. It was this inspiration which sustained Vanini, Hamont, Lewes, Kett, Legate, and Wightman at the stake, and which armed Servetus to prefer the fires of Calvin to the creed of Calvin, which supported Annet in the pillory, and Woolston and Carlile in their imprisonments. It was no capricious taste for negations which dictated these deliberate sacrifices, but a sentiment purer than interest and stronger than self-love—it was the generous passion for unfriended truth.

XII.

The intellectual, no less than the heroic characteristics of Freethought have presented features of obvious unity. Tindal, Shaftesbury, Voltaire, Paine, and Bentham, all vindicated principles of Natural Morality. Shelley struggled that a pure and lofty ideal of life should prevail, and Byron had passionate words of reverence for the human character of Christ.* The distrust of Prayer for temporal help was accompanied by trust in Science, and all saw in material effort an available deliverance from countless ills which the Church can merely deplore. Those who held that a future life was " unproven," taught that attention to this life was of primary importance, at least highly serviceable to humanity, even if a future sphere be certain. All strove for Free Inquiry—Rationalism owed its existence to it; all required Free Speech—Rationalism was diffused by it; all vindicated Free Criticism—Rationalism established itself with it; all demanded to act out their opinions—Rationalism was denuded of conscience without this right. In all its mutations, and aberrations, and conquests, Freethought has uniformly sought the truth, and shown the courage to trust the truth. Freethought uses no persecution, for it fears no opposition, for opposition is its opportunity. It is the cause of Enterprise and Progress, of Reason and Duty —and now seeking the definite and the practical, it selects for its guidance the principle that " human affairs should be regu-

---

* Thus we read, Canto xv. stanza xviii., of Don Juan :—

> Was it not so, great Locke ? and greater Bacon ?
> Great Socrates ? And thou Diviner still
> Whose lot it is by man to be mistaken,
> And thy pure creed made sanctions of all ill ?
> Redeeming world to be by bigots shaken,
> How was thy toil rewarded ?

To this stanza Lord Byron adds this note :—

" As it is necessary in these times to avoid ambiguity, I say that I mean by " Diviner still " CHRIST. If ever God was man—or man God— he was BOTH. I never arraigned his creed, but the use—or abuse—made of it."

† L. H. Holdreth.

lated by considerations purely human."† These—the characteristics which the term Secularism was designed to express—are therefore not inventions, not assumptions, but the general agreements of the Freethought party, inherent, traditional, and historic. That which is new, and of the nature of a development, is the perception that the positivism of Freethought principles should be extended, should be clearly distinguished and made the subject of energetic assertion—that the Freethought party which has so loudly demanded toleration for itself, should be able to exercise it towards all earnest thinkers, and especially towards all co-workers—that those who have protested against the isolation of human effort by sectarian exclusiveness, should themselves set the example of offering, in good faith, practical conditions of unity, not for the glory of sects, or coteries, or schools, but for the immediate service of humanity.

XIII.

The Relation of Secularism to the future demands a few words. To seek after the purity and perfection of the Present Life neither disproves another Life beyond this, nor disqualifies man for it. " Nor is Secularism opposed to the Future so far as that Future belongs to the present world—to determine which we have definite science susceptible of trial and verification. The conditions of a future life being unknown, and there being no imaginable means of benefiting ourselves and others in it except by aiming after present goodness, we shall confessedly gain less towards the happiness of a future life by speculation than by simply devoting ourselves to the energetic improvement of this life."* Men have a right to look beyond this world, but not to overlook it. Men, if they can, may connect themselves with eternity, but they cannot disconnect themselves from humanity without sacrificing duty. Secular knowledge relates to this life. Religious knowledge to another life. Secular instruction teaches the duties to man. Religious instruction the duties to God apart from man. Religious knowledge relates to celestial creeds. Secular knowledge relates to human duties to be performed. The religious teacher instructs us how to please God by creeds. The Secular teacher how to serve man by sympathy and science.

---

* F. W. Newman

Archbishop Whately tells the story of a lady at Bath, who, being afraid to cross a tottering bridge lest it should give way under her, fortunately bethought herself of the expedient of calling for a sedan chair, and was carried over in that conveyance. Some of our critics think that we shall resemble this ingenious lady. But those who fear to trust themselves to the ancient and tottering Biblical bridge, will hardly get into the sedan chair of obsolete orthodoxy, and add the weight of *that* to the danger. They prefer going round by the way of reason and fearless private judgment.

XIV.

Secularism, we have said, concerns itself with four rights :—

1. The right to Think for one's self, which most Christians now admit, at least in theory.

2. The right to Differ, without which the right to think is nothing worth.

3. The right to Assert difference of opinion, without which the right to differ is of no practical use.

4. The right to Debate all vital opinion, without which there is no intellectual equality—no defence against the errors of the state or the pulpit.

It is of no use that the Protestant concedes the right to think unless he concedes the right to differ. We may as well be Catholic unless we are free to dissent. Rome will concede our right to think for ourselves, provided we agree with the Church when we have done ; and when Protestantism affects to award us the right of private judgment, and requires us to agree with the thirty-nine Articles in the end—or when Evangelical Ministers tell us we are free to think for ourselves, but must believe in the Bible nevertheless, both parties reason on the Papist principle ; both mock us with a show of freedom, and impose the reality of mental slavery upon us. It is mere irony to say " Search the Scriptures," when the meaning is—you must accept the Scriptures whether they seem true or not. Of the temper in which theological opinions ought to be formed, we have the instruction of one as eminent as he was capable. Jefferson remarks, " In considering this subject, divest yourself of all bias, shake off all fears and servile prejudices, under which weak minds crouch : fix reason in her seat firmly; question with boldness, even the existence of God ; because, if there be one, he must approve the homage of reason more than that of blindfolded fear. Read the Bible as you would Tacitus or Livy. Those facts in the Bible which contradict the laws of Nature must be examined with care. The New Testament is the history of a person called Jesus. Keep in your eye what is related. They say he was begotten by God, but born of a virgin (how reconcile this?) ; that he was crucified to death, and buried : that he rose and ascended bodily into heaven : thus reversing the laws of Nature. Do not be frightened from this inquiry by any fear, and if it ends in a belief that the story is not true, or that there is not a God, you will find other incitements to virtue and goodness. In fine, lay aside all prejudices on both sides, neither believe nor reject anything because others have rejected or disbelieved it. Your reason is the only oracle given you by heaven, and you are answerable, not for the rightness, but for the uprightness of your opinion : and never mind evangelists, or pseudo-evangelists, who pretend to inspiration."* It is in vain the Christian quotes the Pauline injunction, "Prove all things; hold fast that which is good," if we are to hold fast to his good, which may be evil to us. For a man to prove all things needful, and hold fast to that which he considers good, is the true maxim of freedom and progress. Secularism, therefore, proclaims and justifies the right to Differ, and the right to assert conscientious difference on the platform, through the press, in civil institutions, in Parliament, in courts of law, where it demands that the affirmation of those who reject Christianity shall be as valid as the oath of those who accept it.

XV.

Yet some opponents have professed that Secular cannot be distinguished from Christian rights. Is this so ? The right to think for ourselves has been emphatically and reiteratedly declared to be a Christian right :† it "belongs essentially to Christianity." Now Christianity has no such right. It has the right to think the Bible true, and nothing else. The Christian

---

* "Jefferson : Memoirs." Vol. II. Quoted by Sir G. Cockburn, in his "Confessions of Faith, by a Philosopher," pages 4 and 5.
† "Six Chapters on Secularism," by Dr. Parker, Cavendish Pulpit, Manchester.

has no right to think Christianity untrue, however untrue it may appear. He dare not think it false. He dare no more think it false than the Catholic dare differ from the dictum of the Church, or the Mahomedan differ from the text of the Koran, or the Hindoo differ from the precepts of the Brahmin. Therefore, the Christian's right to think for himself is simply a compulsion to believe. A right implies relative freedom of action ; but the Christian has no freedom. He has no choice but to believe, or perish everlastingly. The Christian right to think for himself is, therefore, not the same as the Secular right. We mean by the right to think, what the term right always implies—freedom and independence, and absence of all crime, or danger of penalty through the honest exercise of thought and maintenance of honest conclusions, whether in favour of or against Christianity. Our assertion is that "Private judgment is free and guiltless." The Christian is good enough to say, we have "a right to think, provided we think rightly." But what does he mean by "rightly?" He means that we should think as he thinks. This is his interpretation of "rightly." Whoever does not fall in with his views, is generally, in his vocabulary, a dishonest perverter of scripture. Now, if we really have the right to differ, we have the right to differ from the Minister or from the Bible, if we see good reason to do so, without being exposed to the censure of our neighbours, or disapprobation of God. The question is not—does man give us the right to think for ourselves ? but, does God give it to us ? If we must come to a given opinion, our private judgment is unnecessary. Let us know at once what we are to believe, that we may believe it at once, and secure safety. If possible disbelief in Christianity will lead to eternal perdition, the right of private judgment is a snare. We had better be without that perilous privilege, and we come to regard the Roman Catholic as penetrative when he paints private judgment as the suggestion of Satan, and the Roman Catholic no less merciful than consistent when he proscribes it altogether. We must feel astonishment at him who declares the Secular right to be essentially a Christian right, when it is quite a different thing, is understood in an entirely different sense, and has an application unknown and unadmitted by Christianity. This is not merely loose thinking, it is reckless thinking.

XVI.

It has been asserted that the second right, "the right to differ," is also a Christian right. "Christianity recognizes the claim to difference of opinion. Christians are not careful to maintain uniformity at the expense of private judgment." This is omitting a part of the truth. Christians often permit difference of opinion upon details, but not upon essentials, and this is the suppression made. The Christian may differ on points of church discipline, but if he differ upon the essential articles of his creed, the minister at once warns him that he is in "danger of the judgment." Let any minister try it himself, and his congregation will soon warn him to depart, and also warn him of that higher Power, who will bid him depart "into outer darkness, where there will be wailing and gnashing of teeth." With respect to the third right, " the right of asserting difference of opinion," this is declared to be not peculiar to Secularism ; that " Christian churches, chapels, literature and services, are so many confirmations of the statement that Christians claim the right of speaking what they think, whether it be affirmative or negative." Yes, so long as what they speak agrees with the Bible. This is the Christian limit ; yet this is the limit which Secularism expressly passes and discards. It is the unfettered right which makes Secularism to differ from Christianity, and to excel it.

XVII.

The right of private judgment, always in set terms conceded to us, means nothing, unless it leads to a new understanding as to the terms in which we are to be addressed. In the " Bible and the People," it is described as " an insolence to ignore Christianity."* We do not understand this language. It would be insolence to Deity to ignore a message which we can recognize as coming from Him, but it may rather imply reverence for God to reject the reports of many who speak in His name. Were we to require Christians to read our books or think as we think, they would resent the requirement as an impertinence ; and we have yet to learn that it is less an impertinence when Christians make these demands of us. If Christians are under no obligation to hold our opinions, neither are we under obligation to hold theirs. By our own

---

* No. 1. Vol. I., p. 8. Edited by the Rev. Brewin Grant.

act, or at their solicitation, we may study " sacred " writings, but at dictation, never ! So long as Secularists obey the laws enacted for the common security, so long as they perform the duties of good citizens, it is nothing to Christians what opinions they hold. We neither seek their counsel nor desire their sentiments—except they concede them on terms of equality. The light by which we walk is sufficient for us ; and as at the last day, of which Christians speak, we shall there have, according to their own showing, to answer for ourselves, we prefer to think for ourselves ; and since they do not propose to take our responsibility, we decline to take their doctrines. Where we are to be responsible, we will be free : and no man shall dictate to us the opinions we shall hold. We shall probably know as well as any Christian how to live with freedom and to die without fear. It is in vain for Christians to tell us that Newton and Locke differed from us. What is that to us unless Newton and Locke will answer for us ? The world may differ from a man, but what is the world to him, unless it will take his place at the judgment-day ? Who is Paul or Apollos, or Matthew or Mark, that we should venture our eternal salvation on his word, any more than on that of a Mahomedan prophet, or a Buddhist priest ? Where the danger is our own, the faith shall be our own. Secularism is not an act conceived in the spirit of pride, or vanity, or self-will, or eccentricity, or singularity, or stiff-neckedness. It is simply well-understood self-defence. If men have the right of private judgment, that right has set them free : and we own no law but reason, no limits but the truth, and have no fear but that of guilt. We may say we believe in honour, which is respecting the truth—in morality, which is acting the truth —in love, which is serving the truth—and in independence, which is defending the truth.

XVIII.

Confucius declared that the foundation of all religion was reverence and obedience.* The Religious sentiment is the intentional reverence of God. The Christian is ever persuaded that there is only one way of doing this, and he arrogantly assumes that he has that way. Whereas the ways are as

---

* Sir John Bowring.

diverse as human genius.   Let those who deny that Secular Truth meets the emotional part of their nature, settle what is the nature of the emotions they desiderate.   The miser wants money—the sensualist wants the cook—the scholar wants knowledge—and the mother desires the life, growth, and happiness of her child.   But what can man want in a rational sense which Nature and humanity may not supply ? Do we not meet the demand of the many when we show that Secularism is sufficient for progress; that it is moral, and therefore suffi- cient for trust; that it builds only upon the known, and is therefore reliable ? It is the highest and most unpresumptuous form of unconscious worship.   It is practical reverence without the arrogance of theoretical homage.   We at least feel con- fident of this, that the future, if it come, will not be miserable. There *may* be a future—this remains to awaken interest and perennial curiosity.   If Nature be conscious, it will still design the happiness of man, which it now permits—this assurance remains, stilling fear and teaching trust.

XIX.

In surveying the position of Christianism in Great Britain, there is found to exist a large outlying class, daily increasing, who for conscientious reasons reject its cardinal tenets.   Hence arises the question :—Are good citizenship and virtuous life on Secular principles, possible to these persons ? Secularism answers, Yes.   To these, excluded by the letter of scripture, by the narrowness of churches, by the intrinsic error and moral repulsiveness of doctrine, Secularism addresses itself ; to these it is the word of Recognition, of Concert and Morality. It points them to an educated conscience as a security of morals, to the study of Nature as a source of help, and seeks to win the indifferent by appeals to the inherent goodness of human Nature and the authority of reason, which Christianism cannot use and dare not trust.   If, however, the Secularist elects to walk by the light of Nature, will he be able to see ? Is the light of Nature a fitful lamp, or a brief torch, which accident may upset, or a gust extinguish ? On the contrary, the light of Nature may burn steady, clear, and full, over the entire field of human life.   On this point we have the testi- mony of an adversary, who was understood to address us, a testimony as remarkable for its quality as for its felicity of expression :—" There is the ethical mind, calm, level, and clear ;

chiefly intent on the good ordering of this life ; judging all things by their tendency to this end, and impatient of every oscillation of our nature that swings beyond it. There is nothing low or unworthy in the attachment which keeps this spirit close to the present world, and watchful for its affairs. It is not a selfish feeling, but often one intensely social and humane, not any mean fascination with mere material interests, but a devotion to justice and right, and an assertion of the sacred authority of human duties and affections. A man thus tempered deals chiefly with this visible life and his comrades in it, because, as nearest to him, they are better known. He plants his standard on the present, as on a vantage ground, where he can survey his field, and manœuvre all his force, and compute the battle he is to fight. Whatever his bearings fervours towards beyond his range, he has no insensibility to the claims that fall within his acknowledged province, and that appeal to him in the native speech of his humanity. He so reverences veracity, honour, and good faith, as to expect them like the daylight, and hears of their violation with a flush of scorn. His word is a rock, and he expects that yours will not be a quicksand. If you are lax, you cannot hope for his trust: but if you are in trouble, you easily move his pity. And the sight of a real oppression, though the sufferer be no ornamental hero, but black, unsightly, and disreputable, suffices perhaps to set him to work for life, that he may expunge the disgrace from the records of mankind. Such men as he constitute for our world its moral centre of gravity; and whoever would compute the path of improvement that has brought it thus far on its way, or trace its sweep into a brighter future, must take account of their steady mass. The effect of this style of thought and taste on the religion of its possessor, is not difficult to trace. It may, no doubt, stop short of avowed and conscious religion altogether ; its basis being simply moral, and its scene temporal, its conditions may be imagined as complete, without any acknowledgment of higher relations."*

XX.

Nature is. That which *is*, is the primary subject of study. The study of Nature reveals the laws of Nature. The laws of

---

* Professor Martineau, in Octagon Chapel, Norwich, 1856.

Nature furnish safe guidance to humanity. Safe guidance is to help available in daily life—to happiness, self-contained—to service, which knows how "to labour and to wait." For authority, Nature refers us to Experience and to Reason. For help, to Science, the nearest available help of man. Science implies disciplined powers on the part of the people, and concert in their use, to realize the security and sufficiency necessary to happiness. Happiness depends on moral, no less than on physical conditions. The moral condition is the full and fearless discharge of Duty. Duty is devotion to the Right. Right is that which is morally expedient. That is morally expedient which is conducive to the happiness of the greatest numbers. The service of others is the practical form of duty; and endurance in the service of others, the highest form of happiness. It is pleasure, peace, security, and desert.

XXI.

We believe there is sufficient soundness in Secular principles to make way in the world. All that is wanted is that advocates of them shall have clear notions of the value of method in their work. To the novice in advocacy policy seems a crime—at least, many so describe it. Unable himself to see his way, the tyro fights at everything and everybody equally; and too vain to own his failure, he declares that the right way. Not knowing that progress is an art, and an art requiring the union of many qualities, he denies all art, cries down policy, and erects blundering into a virtue. Compare the way which Havelock reached Lucknow, and the way in which Sir Colin Campbell performed the same feat, and you see the difference between courage without, and courage with strategy. It was because magnitudes existed, which were inaccessible and incapable of direct measurement, that mathematics arose. Finding direct measurement so often impossible, men were compelled to find means of ascertaining magnitude and distance indirectly. Hence mathematics became a scientific policy. Mathematics is but policy of measurement—grammar but the policy of speech—logic but the policy of reason—arithmetic but the policy of calculation—temperance but the policy of health—trigonometry but the policy of navigation—roads but the policy of transit—music but the policy of controlling sound—art but the policy of beauty—law but the policy of protection—discipline but the policy of strength—love but the policy of affection. An enemy may object to our having a policy, because it suits his purpose that we should be without one; but that a friend should object to our having a policy is one of those incredible infatuations which converts partisans into unconscious traitors. The policy adopted may be a bad policy, and no policy at all is idiotcy. If a policy be bad, criticise and amend it; but to denounce all policy is to commit your cause to the providence of Bedlam. If, therefore, throughout all intelligent control of Nature and humanity, policy is the one supreme mark of wisdom, why should it be dishonourable to study the policy of opinion? He who consistently objects to policy, would build railway engines without safety valves, and dismiss them from stations without drivers; he would abolish turnpike roads and streets, and leave us to find our way at random; he would recommend that vessels be made without helms, and sail without captains, that armies fight without discipline, and artillery-men should fire before loading, and when pointing their guns, should aim at nothing. In fine, a man without policy, honestly and intelligently opposed to policy, would build his house with the roof downwards, and plant his trees with their roots in the air; he would kick his friend and hug his enemy; he would pay wages to servants who would not work, govern without rule, speak without thought, think without reason, act without purpose, be a knave by accident, and a fool by design.

INDEX.